TINY CACTUS PUBLISHING

CLORIST NAME

TEST PAGE

PREPARE YOUR COLOR

WARM UP !!

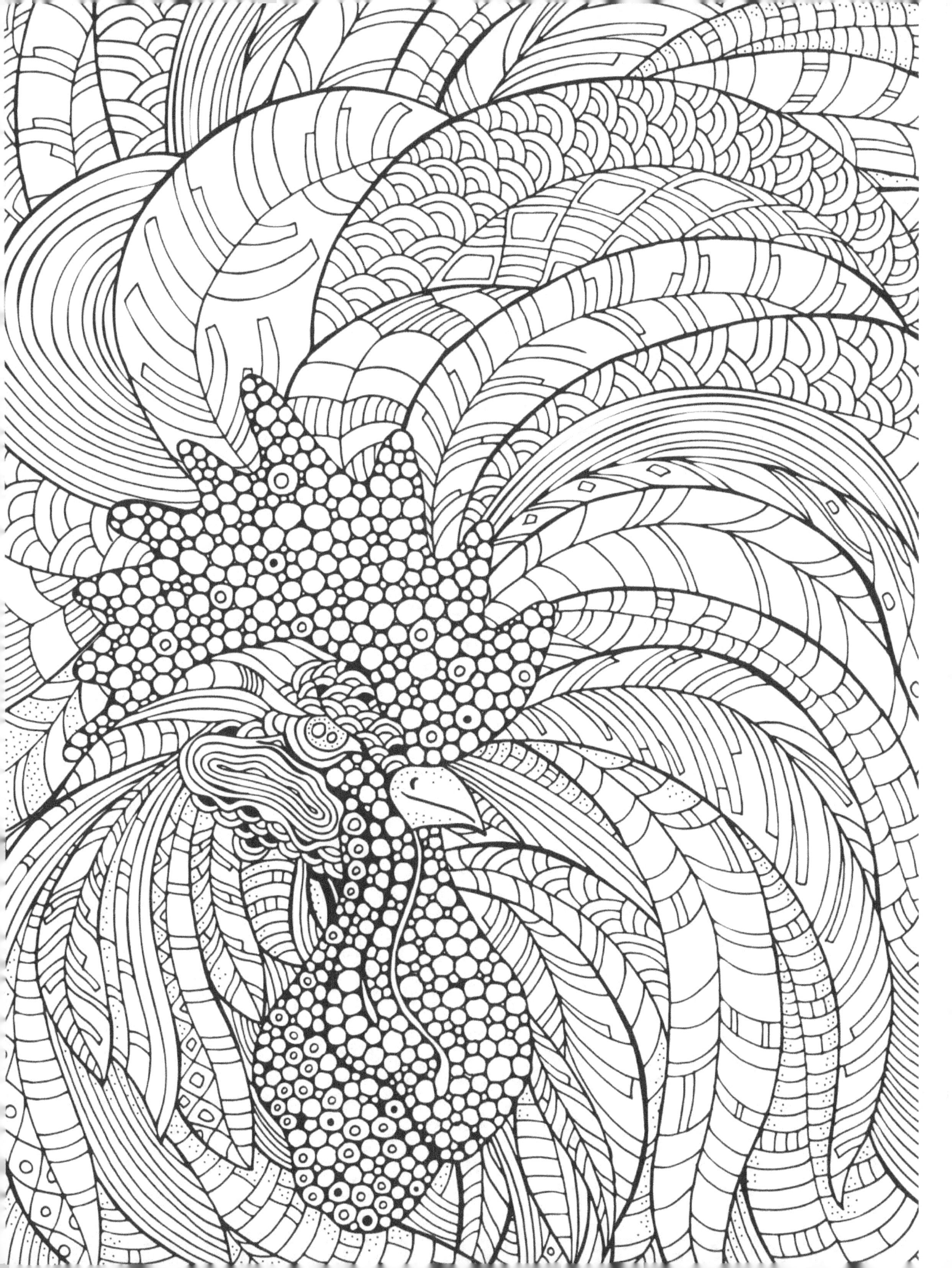

J'aime Paris
Bon Appétit

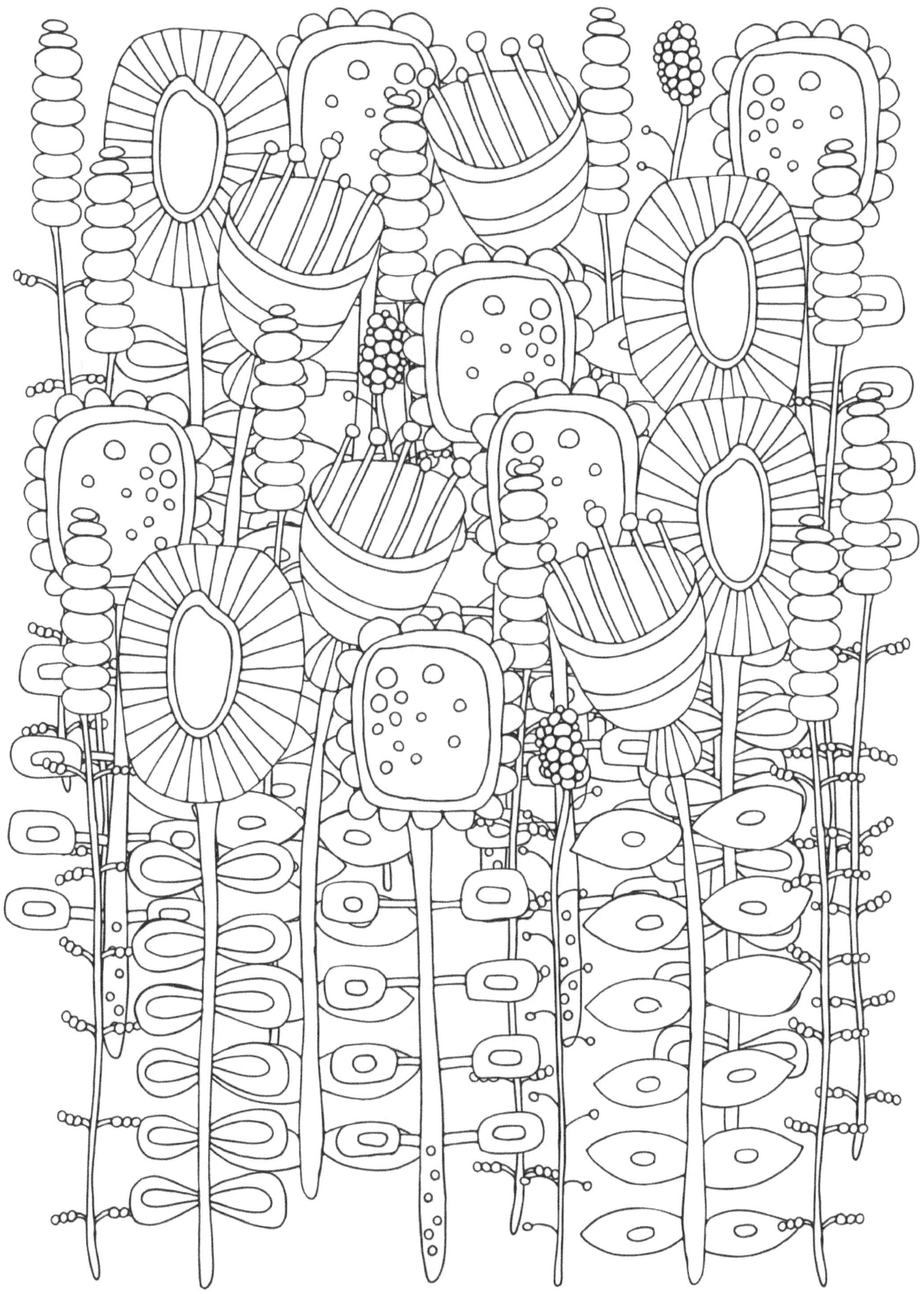

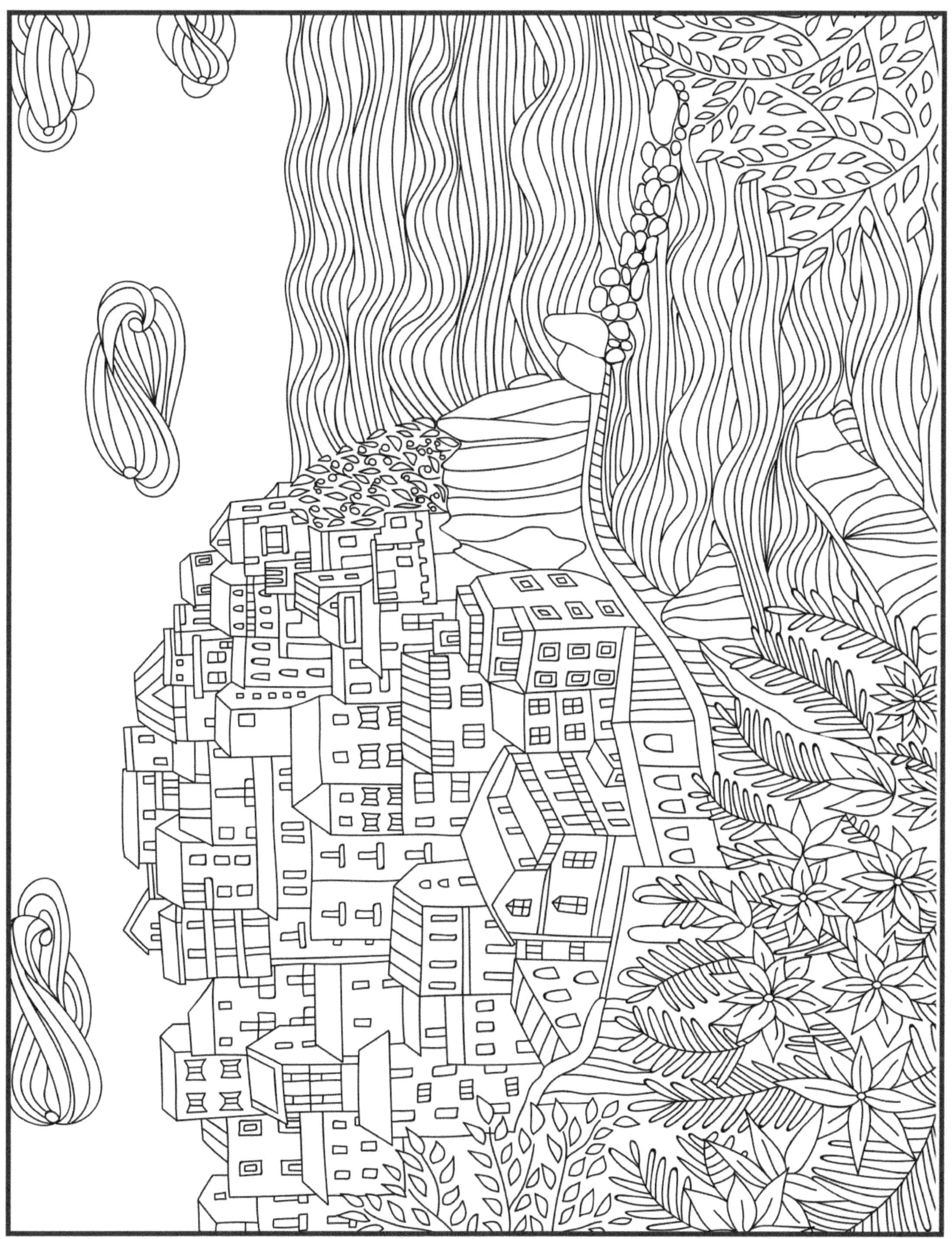

TAXI
NYC
BAGELS

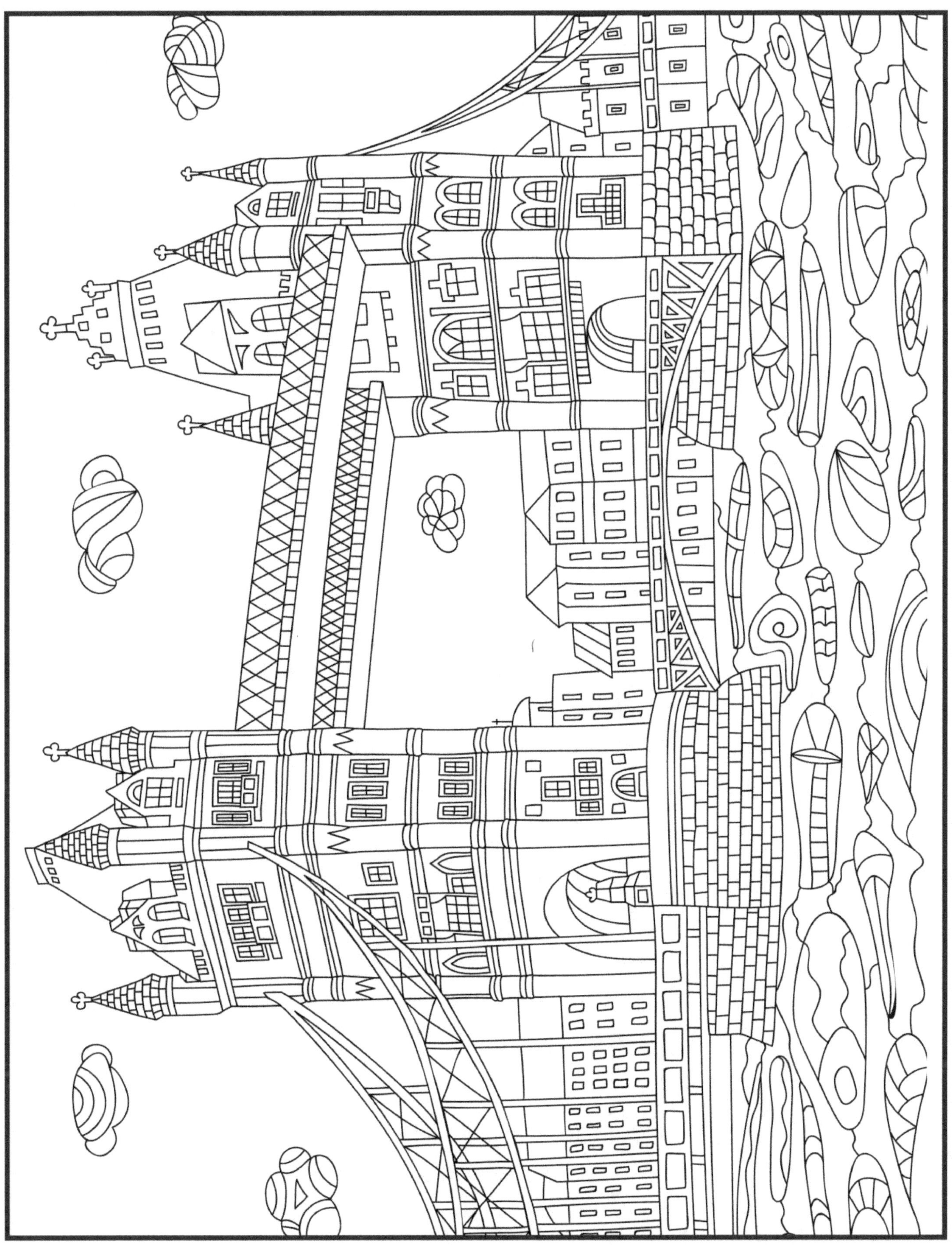

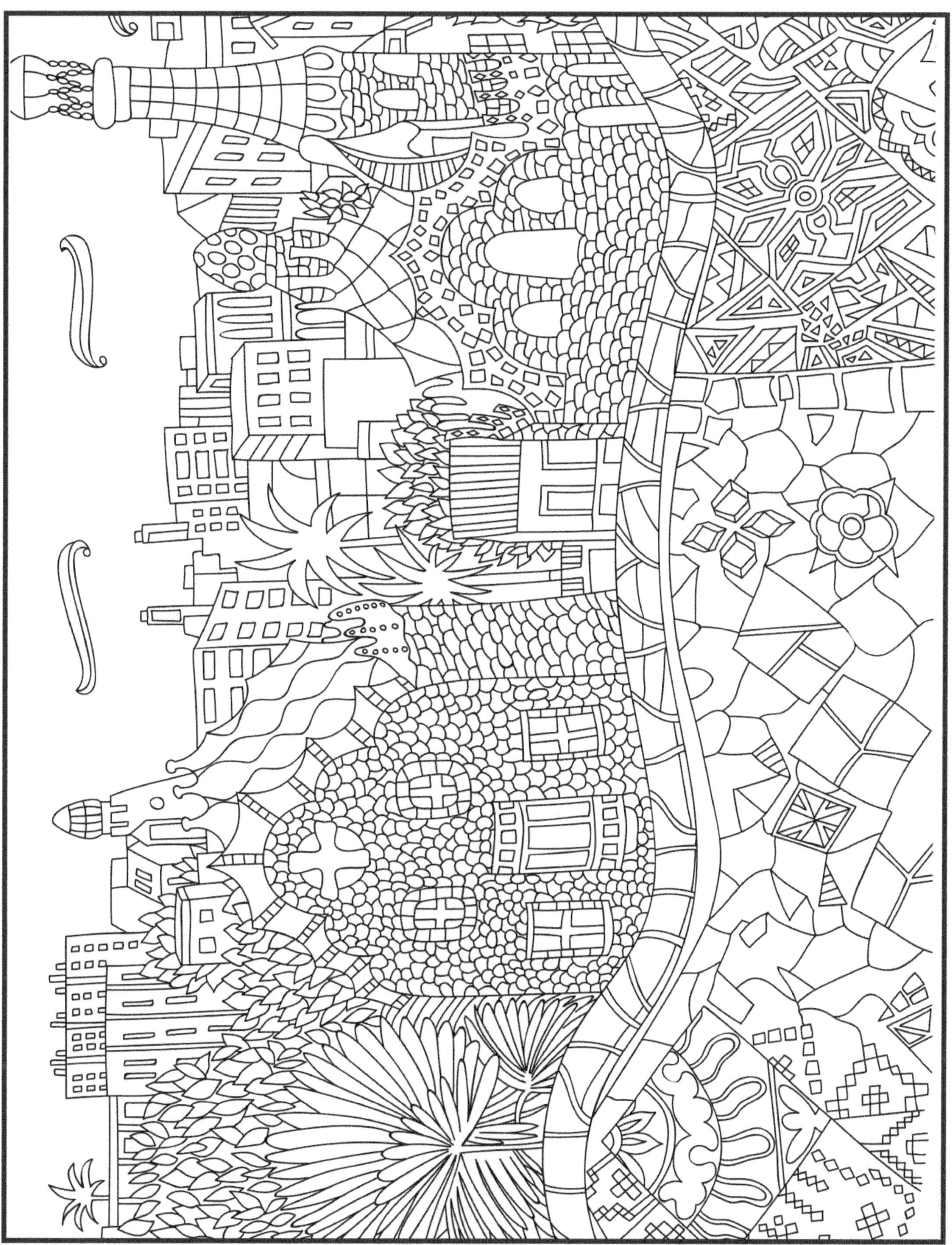

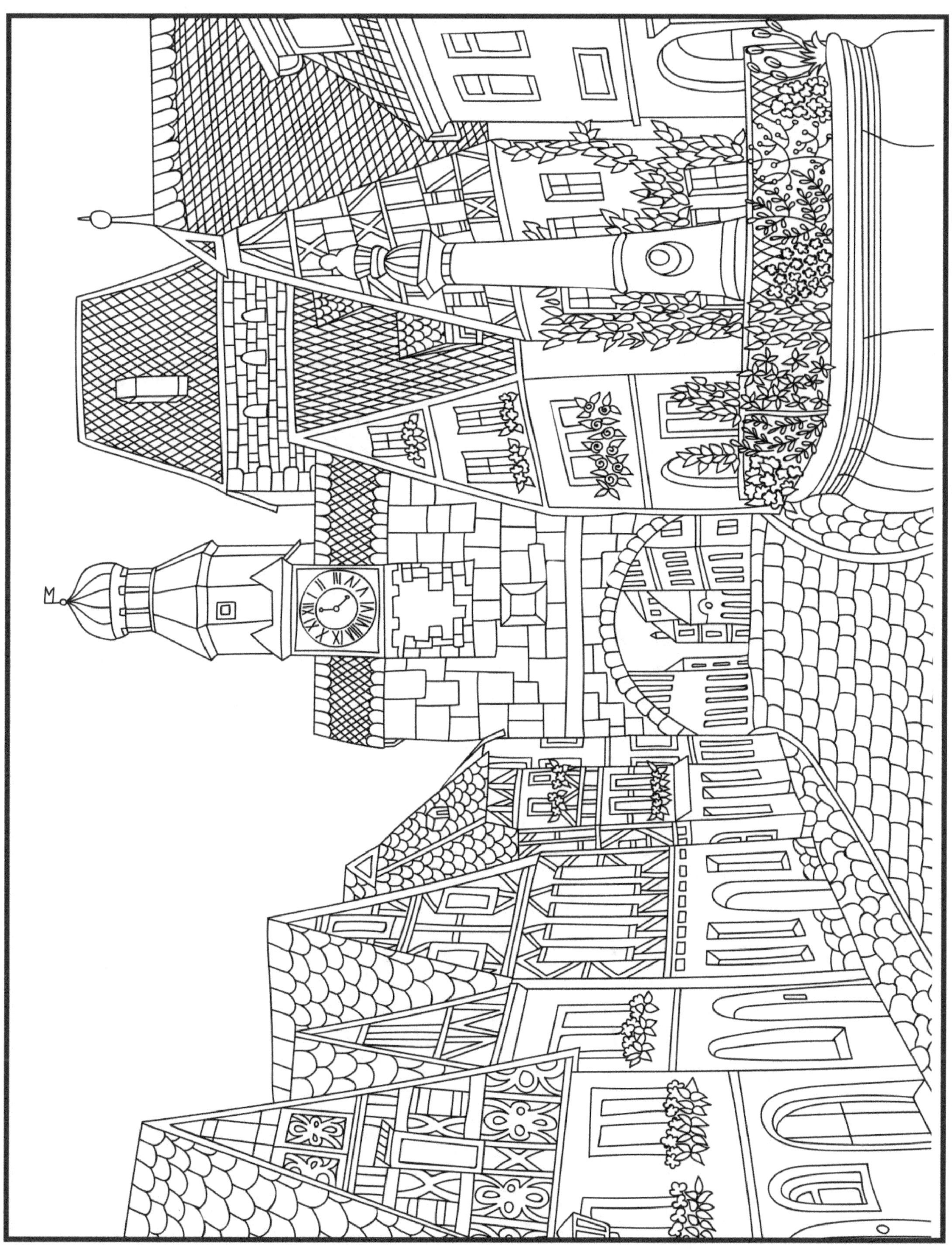

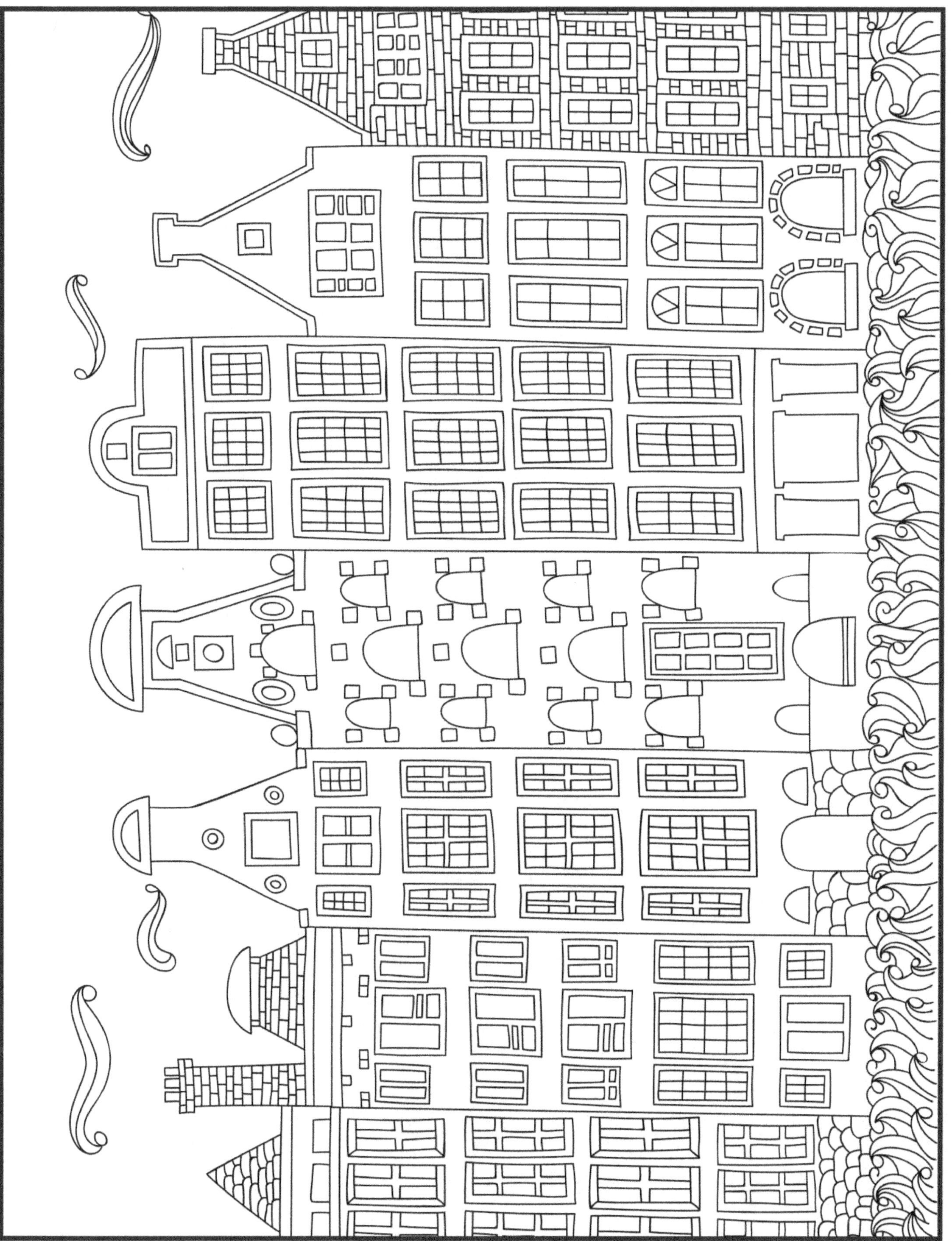

www.ingramcontent.com/pod-product-compliance
Lightning Source LLC
Chambersburg PA
CBHW080814280726
48660CB00018B/3435